All rights reserved. International copyright secured. No part of this book may be reproduced, stored in a retrieval system, or transmitted in any form or by any means—electronic, mechanical, photocopying, recording, or otherwise—without the prior written permission of Learning Engineered Publishing®, a division of Learning Engineered LLC, except for inclusion of brief quotations in an acknowledged review.

Title: *Character Bootcamp*
Subtitle: *A Mission for Boys*

Written by: Christian A. Dickinson
Illustrations by: Learning Engineered LLC

Published by: Learning Engineered Publishing

Library of Congress Control Number: 2026931014
ISBN (Print Hardback): 978-1-965741-53-5

First Edition: 2025

Printed & Created in: United States of America

Text and Illustration Copyright © 2026

Learning Engineered Publishing® (U.S. Reg. No. 8,057,038) is a division of Learning Engineered, LLC, and a subsidiary of Carpe Diem Unlimited Holdings, Inc.

DEDICATION PAGE

For Josh Ward — "JW"

A man of love, strength, steadiness, and grit.
I watched you raise your three boys for a week,
and I saw the kind of father every boy deserves
and every man should strive to become.

Loving.
Firm.
Present.
Unshakeable.

You inspired this book.
Happy 50th Birthday, brother.
This legacy is yours.

CD

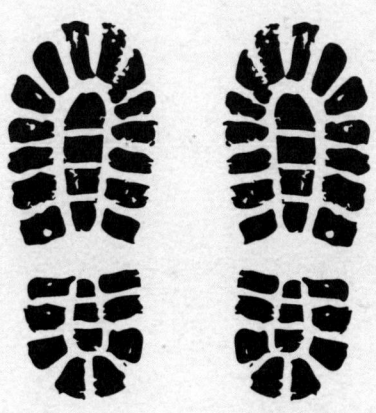

GOD IS WATCHING.
SO AM I.
LET'S ROLL.

— SERGEANT JW

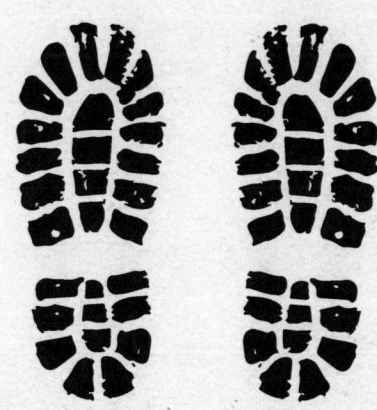

SERGEANT JW

INTRODUCTION

Listen up, recruit.
I'm Sergeant JW.
My orders come straight from Headquarters (that's God).
My mission: shape you into the man He created you to be.
This book is Character Bootcamp.
Ten missions.
Ten of the toughest battles you'll ever fight.
All of them on the inside.
No whining.
No quitting.
No excuses.
You do the mission when nobody's watching—
that's where real muscle grows.
You scared? Good.
Courage isn't the absence of fear.
It's doing the right thing anyway.
Open this book and you've already enlisted.
Close it and walk away… that's your call.
But real men finish what they start.
Turn the page, soldier.
Your first mission is waiting.
Move out!

— Sergeant JW

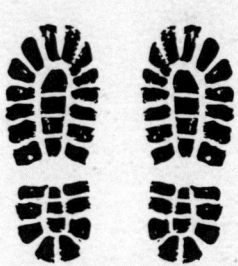

THE RULES

1. One mission at a time. No skipping.
2. Read the Bible verse out loud—God's Word does the heavy lifting.
3. Follow the orders the same day you read them.
4. Take the proof pic—a quick photo showing you did the mission.
    a. Nobody sees it but you and God
    b. No posting
    c. Delete it later if you want.
5. Pray the prayer like you mean it.

Break these rules and you're only cheating yourself.

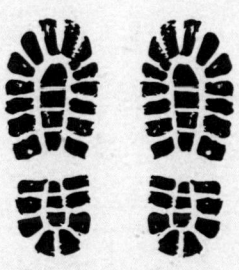

ENLISTMENT

Name: _____

Date: _____

I enter Character Bootcamp today.
Not because I'm perfect—
but because I want to become the man God built me to be.
With God as my witness,
I accept the missions ahead.
No excuses.
No hiding.
No half-effort.
I show up.
I finish.

Signature: _____

Rank: Recruit

Commander-in-Chief: Jesus Christ

This book now belongs to me.
One day, I will pass it on.

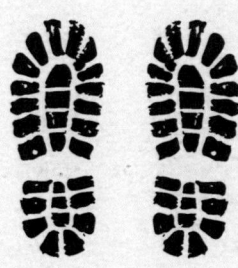

MISSION 1: SELF-CONTROL

DEFINITION: Self-control means being the boss of your body, your mouth, and your temper—even when everything inside wants to take over.

"A person without self-control is like a city whose walls are broken through." —Proverbs 25:28 (NIrV)

TODAY'S ORDERS — OPERATION LOCKDOWN

FOR THE NEXT 24 HOURS:
Zero explosions.
No yelling.
No hitting.
No slamming doors.
No mean words.
When the blow-up rises,
count to five, breathe slow, walk away.

PRAYER
Lord God,
I lose control too fast.
Build strong walls around my heart today.
Fill me with Your strength, not my anger.
Help me stay steady.
Amen.

PROOF OF MISSION
Record the moment you stayed in control.
Mission logged.

MISSION 2: HONOR

DEFINITION: Honor means treating people like they matter—even when they annoy you, correct you, or boss you around. It's respect in your voice. Obedience without attitude. Strength that holds back the comeback.

"Honor your father and mother. Then you will live a long time in the land the Lord your God is giving you."
—Exodus 20:12 (NIrV)

TODAY'S ORDERS — OPERATION YES, SIR

FOR THE NEXT 24 HOURS:
- When an adult gives a direction, respond with respect.
- Do it the first time—no arguing, no excuses.
- Speak respectfully to siblings too.

If you slip, recover fast.
Strong soldiers regain formation.

PRAYER
Lord God,
I talk back too much.
Teach me to honor the people You placed over me.
Help my words stay respectful
and my attitude steady.
Make me a young man of honor.
Amen.

PROOF OF MISSION
Capture one moment of honor.
Carry on, soldier.

MISSION 3: HONESTY

DEFINITION: Honesty means telling the truth—the whole truth—even when it costs you something or makes you look bad.

"The Lord hates those whose lips tell lies. But he is pleased with people who tell the truth."
—Proverbs 12:22 (NIrV)

TODAY'S ORDERS — OPERATION NO COVER

FOR THE NEXT 24 HOURS:
- No lies, big or small.
- No half-truths.
- No silent lies.

If you mess up, own it fast.
Real men fix it.

PRAYER
Lord God,
lying feels easier, but it makes me weak.
Give me the guts to tell the truth today,
no matter what.
Make my words straight and clean.
Amen.

PROOF OF MISSION
Record the moment you told the truth when it hurt.
Mission logged.

MISSION 4: PURITY

DEFINITION: Purity means keeping your eyes, mind, and body clean—because they belong to God, not to the world.

"How can a young person keep their way pure?
By living according to your word." —Psalm 119:9 (NIrV)

TODAY'S ORDERS — OPERATION CLEAN GUARD

FOR THE NEXT 24 HOURS:
- Look away immediately.
- Shut it down.
- Walk out.
- Change the chat.
- No second looks.
- No excuses.

Your eyes are on my watch, soldier.

PRAYER
Lord God,
the world throws filth at me every day.
Give me strength to bounce my eyes
and guard my heart like a fortress.
Keep me clean for You.
Amen.

PROOF OF MISSION
Record the moment you turned away or shut it down.
Mission logged.

MISSION 5: COURAGE

DEFINITION: Courage means doing the right thing even when your stomach is in knots and everyone else runs the other way.

"Be strong and brave.
Do not be afraid.
Do not lose hope."
—Joshua 1:9 (NIrV)

TODAY'S ORDERS — OPERATION STAND FIRM

FOR THE NEXT 24 HOURS:
- Do one hard right thing that scares you.
- Stand up for someone.
- Admit your mistake.
- Say no when the group wants you to sin.

Fear is allowed.
Running is not.

PRAYER
Lord God,
my knees shake,
but I want to be brave for You.
Go with me today.
Give me Your courage.
Amen.

PROOF OF MISSION
Record the moment you stood when you wanted to run.

MISSION 6: TAMING THE TONGUE

DEFINITION: Taming the tongue means keeping your words clean, kind, and under control—no cursing, trash talk, gossip, or tearing others down.

"Praise and cursing come out of the same mouth.
My brothers and sisters, it shouldn't be that way."
—James 3:10 (NIrV)

TODAY'S ORDERS — OPERATION SILENT WEAPON

FOR THE NEXT 24 HOURS:
- Zero curse words.
- Zero put-downs.
- Zero gossip.

If nothing good to say—zip it.

PRAYER
Lord God,
my mouth gets me in trouble every day.
Put Your guard on my lips.
Help me speak life, not poison.
Amen.

PROOF OF MISSION
Record the moment you bit your tongue instead of blasting someone.
Mission logged.

MISSION 7: ANGER MANAGEMENT

DEFINITION: Anger management means being slow to get mad and quick to let it go—
refusing to sin when you're angry.

"When you are angry, do not sin.
Do not let the sun go down while you are still angry."
—Ephesians 4:26 (NIrV)

TODAY'S ORDERS — OPERATION COOL DOWN

FOR THE NEXT 24 HOURS:
- Feel the anger, but don't feed it.
- No revenge.
- No grudges.

If you blow it, apologize fast
and kill the anger before bedtime.

PRAYER
Lord God,
anger feels strong but it makes me weak.
Teach me to hand it to You instead of swinging.
Cool my heart today.
Amen.

PROOF OF MISSION
Record the moment you let it go instead of feeding the fire.
Mission logged.

MISSION 8: HUMILITY

DEFINITION: Humility means knowing you're not the center of the universe—
win without bragging,
lose without whining,
serve without needing credit.

"Be humble.
Value others more than yourselves."
—Philippians 2:3 (NIrV)

TODAY'S ORDERS — OPERATION INVISIBLE

FOR THE NEXT 24 HOURS:
- Let someone else go first.
- Say "good job" when they beat you.
- Do a job nobody will notice or thank you for.

PRAYER
Lord Jesus,
You washed feet.
Kill my pride
and teach me to serve like You.
Make me small in my own eyes today.
Amen.

PROOF OF MISSION
Record the moment you stepped back so someone else could shine.
Mission logged.

MISSION 9: RESPONSIBILITY

DEFINITION: Responsibility means doing what you're supposed to do when you're supposed to do it—
without being nagged or reminded.

"Whoever can be trusted with very little
can also be trusted with a lot."
—Luke 16:10a (NIrV)

TODAY'S ORDERS — OPERATION OWN IT

FOR THE NEXT 24 HOURS:
- Do every job, chore, and assignment
- the first time—
- no reminders,
- no excuses,
- no "in a minute."

PRAYER
Lord God,
I dodge what's mine too often.
Give me strength to own my duties today like a man.
No shortcuts.
Amen.

PROOF OF MISSION
Record the moment you did the job before anyone told you.
Mission logged.

MISSION 10: INTEGRITY

DEFINITION: Integrity means doing the right thing when nobody's watching and nobody will ever know.

"You know when I sit down and when I get up. You know what I'm thinking."
—Psalm 139:2 (NIrV)

TODAY'S ORDERS — OPERATION SOLO WATCH

FOR THE NEXT 24 HOURS:
- Do the right thing in every hidden moment—
- phone alone,
- empty house,
- no one checking.
- Because God always sees.

PRAYER
Lord God,
You see everything.
Help me live today
like the man I want to be tomorrow—
even in the dark.
Make me solid through and through.
Amen.

PROOF OF MISSION
Record the moment only God and you will ever know about.
Mission logged.

You completed the course.

Most recruits quit.

You didn't.

Headquarters has a new set of orders for you…

but those come later.

For now, stand tall.

You are no longer just a boy.

You are dangerous to the enemy.

And you are watched with pride from above.

— Sergeant JW

P.S. Burn this page. Real men don't need proof.

www.ingramcontent.com/pod-product-compliance
Lightning Source LLC
Chambersburg PA
CBRC091209010526
44107CB00022B/1267